Whispers Through the Mist of Time

by

Filomena T. Troso

DIAMOND MEDIA PRESS CO.
1-304-460-1427
https://www.diamondmediapressco.com/

Copyright © **2023**

By **Filomena T. Troso**

All rights reserved.

No part of this book may be used or reproduced by any means, graphic, electronic, or mechanical, including photocopying, recording, taping or by any information storage retrieval system without the written permission of the author except in the case of brief quotations embodied in critical articles and reviews.

The views expressed in this work are solely those of the author and do not necessarily reflect the views of the publisher, and the publisher hereby disclaims any responsibility for them.

Any people depicted in stock imagery provided by Thinkstock are models, and such images are being used for illustrative purposes only. Certain stock imagery @Thinkstock.

ISBN Paperback: 978-1-7333011-2-1

WHISPERS THROUGH THE MIST OF TIME

Grumo Appula, my birthplace.

Dedication

To my daughter, Venus and my husband Joseph for all their encouragement.

The author in a field of daisies.

Contents

INTRODUCTION

The Town — Roccavivara
The Country — Italy
Time-Past / Present

A LONG TIME AGO; it seems like yesterday...
Strange, how this logic collides.

In a lotus position I close my eyes to immerse my senses in moments of my favorite memories. Drifting off into the vault of what was; leaving the present temporarily behind I hear the magical sound of Church bells tolling, filtering trough the fog of time as the sounds slowly gains momentum!

I give myself completely into inner visions of years gone by,

I see the Piazza so clearly that I can almost smell the bread baking in someone's home nearby.

I hear the water splashing from the ever flowing fountain, people going about their lives fetching water from the fountain in the piazza, ladies dressed in black with scarves upon their heads and rosary in hand going to church.

A baby in its mother's arms suckling on her breast as she looks on at her babe with adoring eyes while softly caressing him.

Children at play, including my two little brothers Leo and Franco their laughter bubbling out of them like the sound of water splashing as it hits the stones around the base of the fountain.

My friend Olga was beautiful, with golden hair fashioned into braids that crossed at the nape of her neck and wrapped around her head with pins to keep it all in place. She lived behind our house where we lived. Olga's father was a strange benevolent man. He was always barefooted and liked to put his head under the running water ritualistically everyday; even when it was cold, brrrr.

The only time he was not seen out was when it snowed, that was wise of him.

He was a tall thin man and never spoke much; in fact as I think about it I don't recall ever hearing his voice. He had a lot of curly white hair, from too much water? I always wondered. He was thought to be not all together, but he was part of the whole pie. None of the children ridiculed him instead they played with him and he with them.

The sound of sheep bells assault me I see a family friend bring in their sheep from the field. (Most homes had built in stalls/barns under their homes for their chickens and other domestic animals.)

I can almost see and hear them as in a dream come alive.

I hear the music of an accordion rolling in from the mist of time being played by a peasant taking a break from his work, he played a soft folk melody of love that was lost to him; ah love.

Always of love, the only other exception was religious songs; my favorite was La Madonna Di Monte Vergine. It was special because the town folks joined in the vocals as in a chant; and as I reflect, I realized that it was perfect in it's imperfection which made it what it was...memorable.

The melodious song added to this magical moment and was carried by the winds of fate to safely reach my earnest ears to be stored in my heart forever.

As I continued on the journey as a voyeur through the window of time, my senses became flooded of it all and I felt that I actually was there in spirit if not physically.

The splashing, laughter, and tolling of the bells all became one; each kept their individual sounds...But together; it was a magnificent symphony of the senses...

The accordion was like a big dollop of whipped cream on a sundae of memories.

The Church bells have a rich resonant sound, loud but with a hypnotic pleasant delivery that infiltrated every cranny of the village.

My heart and beyond, in fact the village on top of the nearest mountain of San Giovanni could hear our Church bells I am certain, as we could hear theirs especially on their Patron Saints Holiday and fireworks, visually as well.

The feelings of nostalgic remembrance leaves me delighted beyond words,

Yet the joy I feel for that special place in my heart is almost too great to bear.

Too much joy can also be painful...

The lack of money only lend to the simple joys derived from not having materialistic means.

The simplicity synonymous with innocence leaves me breathless and in awe, that a time such as that actually existed in my lifetime and I was part of it all.

I am fortunate and blessed to have those memories of my home when I was a child. In a sense we do step back in time, we feel what we felt.

The joys and the many small things of every day life in the simplest form of a bygone era, fills my heart, knowing that my footsteps left behind will forever be stamped on the earth of Roccavivara.

Memories... like a spring shower upon the garden of life.

Good imagination teamed with positive loving attitude can conquer adversities. Believe and it shall.

I hope you enjoy these wonderful recollections of my life as I remember them.

My Visions / Dreams are all true experiences.

–Filomena Tina Troso

Mena

Bits and pieces of things remembered vividly

THE YEAR WAS 1944 IN ITALY. Evidence of destruction from the war was everywhere. The men who survived, in a daze, were slowly trickling back to their families. One of the many men that never returned was Mena's uncle, Aunt Angelina's husband.

Mena was a beautiful child of golden curls, and a pouty small mouth, with large dark expressive eyes and a face that resembled the cherubs in Michelangelo's paintings.

Mena was in a covered wagon with a donkey driven by her father. Her mother and older brother Cesarino were inside, along with her mother's younger brother, uncle Mario. The old wagon was acquired from a traveling circus by the bartering of a watch, and the small stubborn *asinello* (small donkey) by a palm reading of the entire family. You can imagine how colorful the wooden wagon must have been as they went through the small towns on the way to the village where mamma was from, and where her grandparents lived in the Molise region.

That night to avoid attention her Papa' smeared mud all over the colorful letters, until the thunderous rain came down in buckets.

It took longer to get there because of the torrential rain they had to deal with, and the temperamental asinello which made it difficult to travel.

The tires got stuck in the mud several times, and many times as the asinello refused to move. The Nazis had been seen in the surrounding areas. They had been warned by different farmers, and were offered lodging and food. They gratefully accepted their hospitality, and left before daylight.

Her father was cranky, because of the difficult journey. Mena was also cranky, because she just wanted to go back to sleep. Dawn was breaking and there were birds chirping as it welcomed the new day. The sun's rays brought everything alive and covered all its surrounding with a golden glow. The majestic cross, surrounded with wild flowers, was a sight to behold. The mist surrounding the base of the village slowly dissipated and the beautiful sight magically emerged from the mist, appearing into view atop the mountain. The Church steeple in the center was a welcoming sight.

Her grandparents warmly welcomed them with a wonderful meal of a big round loaf of homemade bread with hot peppers and cheese, which they devoured with gusto. They had also arranged for them to stay in a very nice dwelling, steps from the piazza and the fountain.

They soon settled in their home.

A few months later on a cold day, a large man barged into their home.

He stood in front of the opened door blocking the light, and demanded, "ova, ova" (eggs, eggs) while pointing his long firearm at her mamma.

He looked dark, like a big bear.

We could not see his face because of the sunlight behind him.

Mena ran behind her mamma and grabbed her skirt, and would not let go. She became part of her skirt, frightened, while peeking trying not to look at him. Her mamma moved slowly to the table and removed a cloth uncovering a loaf of bread, offered it to him saying, "no ova, pane si'ecco". (No eggs, we have bread here). He grabbed the bread and ran out abruptly. The sunlight poured in giving light to a very dark moment. Mamma held Mena, sat and cried for a long time.

Haystacks were being burned throughout the surrounding farmlands, animals were stolen and young women were raped.

The few men that were left and the ones that managed to escape the horror of war hid, and rightly so or they would have been shot on sight if seen.

Years later we learned an affirmation of rumors that the men took care of matters in their own hands, to protect their families.

Messengers were scattered, the Nazis could not reach all the way up to the village without being bombarded with stones, and they had an abundance of them. Consequently very few made it to the top.

But some still made it!

It was spring, the sounds of nature in its full abandon filtered through the open windows, which gave comfort as she tried to nap.

Everyone napped in the afternoon. She wasn't quite asleep yet, when she saw the shadow of a man coming towards her! Something was wrong! Very bad, wrong. She made believe she was sleeping!

The birds were loud and sounded scary now...

She heard her mother's footsteps come up the stairs, and as she entered the room, she instinctively took that moment to run out of the room leaving behind loud angry voices. Almost tripping as she ran down the stairs, and out the door, she kept running...

She felt bad, because she thought her mother was angry with her, as tears stung her eyes and made it difficult to see, till she forgot what she was running from. Beautiful red poppies were everywhere. She picked some.

She could see right through them.

Then she saw the beautiful butterflies. They were like a rainbow of changing colors, as the sun caressed their fluttering wings of blue and gold. She wanted to be a butterfly.

She began to follow them as they beckoned her to chase them through the grass and trees. They would hide from her, and then re-appear as if out of nowhere.

The game went on for a long time as she wandered off.

There were many butterflies, white ones, blue ones, and golden ones too, down the slope of the hill where the grass was high and no one could see them play. She liked it here!

It was getting dark, and she was getting hungry. Someone was calling her!

Birds fluttered away toward the blue sky, startled as she was by the angry voice calling her. She did not answer; she wanted to stay here with the butterflies, of blue and gold, birds, and soft little rabbits, among many others.

Crawly things, small things, that wanted to play as she chased them.

Her father found her! With force he grabbed her by the arm, while angrily scolding her... pulling her along the clearing.

Her arm hurt, and she stun1bled while running, as she tried to keep up.

When they got home, she was to sit on a chair quietly and watch everyone eat.

Sobs came in gulps as tears flowed. She was hungry and had to go to potty but didn't really want to go because it burned when she did. She thought about the blue and golden butterflies and stopped for a moment, then resumed crying, until she couldn't catch her breath.

Her mother came to wipe her nose. Her father didn't like that, and scolded her too. Discipline, you know. Mena was three years young. Even as a child, Mena knew how to periodically escape into a world of serenity and beauty, as the world around her faded from reality!

She'd go to a field of red poppies and butterflies of blue and gold. She closed her eyes, and became one them.

She would stare at an object that caught her eye, a sparkle on a glass or anything that had designs and color. She could make out things in it, even saw a dog, and a bird once, and faces... many faces; smiling faces everywhere, and then they'd disappear. But they always came back when she looked for them. Sometimes the faces looked angry; she then would push them away with the poppies tune, and the faces became butterflies.

In the sunlight her mother's hair had rainbow colors in it. She would lose herself in those beautiful colors. As she grew older, Mena had adversity in her young life; as she remembered with trepidations that cold day of spring, with the beautiful butterflies in the grassy field of red poppies tall and bright.

Mena's father was a traveling photographer. Michele was a handsome charismatic man of small to medium stature, with dark wavy hair and mustache, and dark hypnotic eyes.

Everyone liked him, especially in the small village in the mountains. He was a city man. He spoke without a dialect, and people respected that.

He liked everything to be perfect, which made her mother miserable, as she was the opposite. She was a beautiful, earthy, rosy- cheeked slightly robust country girl, with light brown hair and deep-set eyes of blue-green-gray, with an hourglass figure, and could never please him.

Her name was Concetta Sallustio.

He used to tell friends with a smile that when it rained he would seek shelter under her bosoms. She always smiled back amused.

When the war was over, Michele had enough of the small village living, and moved his family back to the town of Grumo Appula, west of Bari, a seaport city on the Adriatic Seacoast, where she and her brother were born. They temporarily stayed with Michele's maternal uncle Peppino and his wife Camilla. They had a photography studio, which doubled as their living quarters in the back, and beyond that was the darkroom where he processed photos.

Mena had been there before. She did not want to think about it, instead she went into a trance and started to hum "butterflies of blue and gold play with me, I have wings, and we will fly. Papaveri, (poppies) they are bright red and so tall, and I am so little."

"Italian:"

Tu sai che I papaveri sono alti-alti-alti

E tu sei piccolina, e tu sei piccolina...

In a sing-song tune, she remembered this from a long time ago.

Mena at 2

Mena at 3

My parents, Michele and Concetta

Dreams One

DREAMS, WHAT ARE DREAMS; why do we have them? The experts tell us it is a necessary phenomenon. Even when we have no recollection of ever having one, we have them. But what about nightmares that come alive in a surrealistic movie setting, that you unwillingly have?

God help you if it's a nightmare.

Could they be a warning? Or better still, a message from beyond—a glimpse from things to be?

Things you would not even remotely think of! A past life, a memory, or perhaps...

A connection with another, living or departed... Who knows?

Here is an example of a dream I had.

One cold winter night in Wheeling, Illinois I was awakened by a scratching at the door.

I hastened down the stairs and opened the door. To my amazement and shock, there stood my sweet little sheltie dog Prince, "Princey poo" as my daughter and I affectionately called him. Disheveled and shivering, I immediately scooped him up, wrapped him in a towel and placed him at the foot of my bed, and went back to sleep.

The next morning I was puzzled and disturbed by my dream.

But no matter, it was just a dream after all.

A month before, my daughter, Prince, and I drove to Alexandria

Virginia to visit my in-laws. My husband was working in Washington D.C., area at the time and was staying with his parents in Alexandria.

Two weeks later we drove back home, as my daughter Venus was due back in school. We left Prince with my husband to keep him company on his drive home, which was to take place in less then a month—hopefully, he said.

I could not shrug off the memory of my dream. It seemed so real! Was this a premonition? My mother had them; as well as my grandmother. With trepidation I called my husband, John (now x-husband), and asked how Prince was coping being away from us and told him that I had a disturbing dream the night before.

"Tell me what you dreamed," he asked.

He was quiet as he listened—too quiet! With a touch of hesitation, he aid, "He's fine, don't worry." I was worried, but maybe I overreacted, so I brushed it aside

A month and a half later, my daughter Venus and I drove to Alexandria again. John was still tied up in his work and had not been able to come home.

Two days later, my daughter screamed out "Prince is dyiiiing... Mommyyyy!"

I rushed to the living room and saw Prince on his back having a seizure. I quickly called a vet for advice, calmed my daughter, and put something in the dog's mouth.

When my husband got home I asked him, "What happened to Prince, he never had seizures before?"

He said,"Do you remember when you called about the dream you had about him? Well the day before he ran out and got hit by an ambulance and was in the animal hospital, I didn't want to upset you and Venus, plus the vet told me he would be fine in a few days, but I'm glad you girls didn't ask to speak to him."

"That's not funny, Dad," Venus replied in a loud voice from her room.

Prince survived a long life with occasional seizures. We loved that dog.

Visions

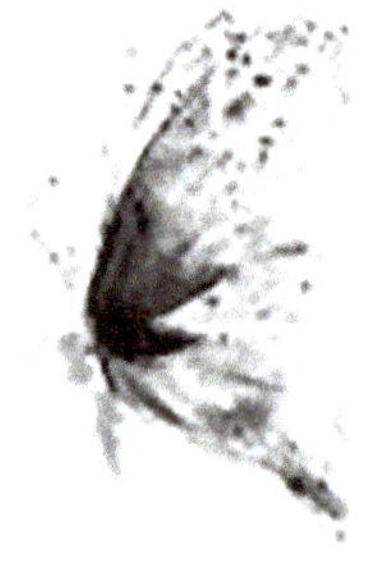

ONE EVENING IN THE FALL, a missionary was scheduled to speak in our church. Our music director George and several of our choir member friends highly recommended that we attend. We all waited with anticipation to hear this knowledgeable pious man.

We sat in the fifth row in the center and listened. He was truly remarkable.

The back of the altar in the Holy Name of Jesus Church is made of stones, with the figure of Jesus in the center, elevated, which gives the appearance of Jesus floating with his arms lovingly outstretched.

I listened with my heart open as my eyes wandered to the figure of Jesus and to the stonework behind him. Then to my amazement, I saw it. I nudged my husband, "Look ...look, on the left side in the middle." I couldn't believe it. I looked away to make sure it was still there!

It was! I blinked, and then I looked away again... It did not fade into the stone formation. I looked in a different section, but the vision of my mother's face was clearly etched in the stone. Facing her was the figure of a man with a hat—his face was not revealed to me.

But I know it might have been my father; I do not recall my father ever wearing a hat, however.

He passed away in 1951 and my mother in 2005.

During the following months I tried to recreate the same mode of environment, you know, same time, same row, hoping to recapture the vision of my mother...to no avail. Perhaps someday, or perhaps some things are only meant to come into your life....but once!

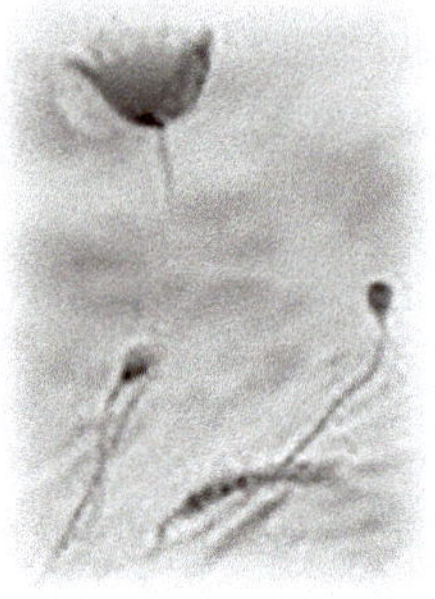

Dreams, we all have them. Throughout history it shows substantial belief in its prophetic accuracy. The famine of Egypt and other disasters that followed were seen in a vision/dream.

I was ten years young and lived with my mother along with my two younger brothers, Dinuccio and Franchino. Let me tell you how those names came to be! Dinuccio was named after my uncle Leopoldo-Leopoldino Dino=Dinuccio. But here in America he is "Leo." Franchino was named after our great-grandfather Francesco, thus Franco-Franchino and, of course, here he is called "Frank." In fact he legally changed it.

At this time I lived in Roccavivara. My father was in a sanitarium with consumption in Reggio Emilia. Although my mother had not seen him for a long time, they had separated, but she always prayed for him.

I went to see Mrs. Cirulli's baby and played with him for a while. He was adorable and was always happy to see me. Don Nicola (the grandfather) asked if I would go fetch a bottle of wine for that evening's dinner.

The basement is where the cheese and sausages were kept to age and conserve. The wine was kept in the sub basement where it was cooler.

I merrily skipped down the stairs, when I heard someone calling my name, "Filomena." I stopped in my tracks. I knew that voice. Where was it coming from? Nonsense... I had to fetch the wine. One more flight of stairs; then I heard it again, "Filomena." I froze! At this point all I wanted to do was to be out of there...

I ran up the steps and out the door where I burst out in the sunshine.

The incident was soon forgotten. I ran all the way to the bottom of the town where my Nanna lived. I spend the rest of the afternoon picking figs from the big fig tree in my Nanna's back yard.

I liked being with her. We made dolls out of the dried figs from the windowsills where they were kept to dry.

Later that afternoon I headed for home, after chatting with some neighbors, and as I approached home I was startled to see a crowd near our front door. My brothers saw me and ran to me, "Papa' is dead, Papa' is dead... Mamma got a telegram." I stood there speechless! The figs tumbled down from my skirt, which I used to hold them, skipping and bouncing off of the cobblestones as they fell in slow motion along with my fig dolls. They looked like they were dancing to the music of an accordion playing from a distance.

I was going to tell Mamma about the voice, but not now. Later I will.

I never did...I wish I had!

Reflection (Dream)

In a park with lots of trees

MANY PEOPLE, PEOPLE watching people going about as if
They weren't. So was I.
Without warning I felt a strong sense of frustration and anger.
Where was it coming from?
The hurt and degradation I felt was pulling me down to my knees.
I was drawn towards a dark thin man in his middle years
Sitting on a bench alone, he wore a cap and was dressed in brown
shabby clothes.
The hurt was unbearable, I felt it! He was in my head.
He was hurt, had been hurt, I knew what was in his heart.
I was compelled to go to him.
I sat next to him; he was not surprised, almost as if he was expecting
me.
We spoke for a long time,
His features slowly softened.
I told him how could he hate with so much venom
When he had a granddaughter white as a lily!
Who absolutely adored him, and how could he feel hate for anyone

If...he chose to see part of himself in them.
Somehow everything seemed to change,
As he realized that his anger/anguish was misguided and misplaced.
The hurt caused by hate!
A burden now released and understood for what it was.

Strange Dreams (Fear)

GREAT DAY, FEELING GOOD, it was spring, and I was out for a happy walk. The birds were enjoying the day as much as I was, and squirrels were chasing each other. All the trees were bringing forth new life; a beautiful glorious day indeed.

At last my life seemed to have fallen in order, I felt happy and at peace.

Until, during my walk, I looked to my right and between two buildings was an empty space with a fence and some shrubbery in the back. The building on the right was a narrow two-story white house. The other was decrepit and looked abandoned-and there it was, with the shrubbery behind him. Between the houses, with the upper part erect and the bottom part of its body coiled.

A bald, round head, with a face of pure evil. All the hate in the human race must have been gathered reflected and stamped in that grotesque miniature face with the body of a... PYTHON!

Our eyes met. I felt the hate pour out of it, as in a black engorged river of hate. I froze in pure terror... It froze too, for a nano second. But, somehow in that second, I felt that he was afraid of me as well. I broke away from his hateful glare and I ran to the white house and prayed that the door was open. It was.

The door opened; I ran in and locked it behind me. I stood there with my back to the door, arms outstretched. I looked up and whispered, "I'm safe! He has no hands!"

I woke up bathed in perspiration.

Note:

A fight of wits, between good and evil?

Strange Dream (Betrayed)

I WAITED TILL DARK; I could not risk going out during the day. It seems that even old friends betrayed one another these days, to remain protected. For a while anyway! I felt completely alone in the quest for survival...And I was truly a survivor.

I must try to reach Tonino. He lives a few miles from the village in a farm that was owned by his great grandfather. When we were children we used to play together even though he was several years older. It was in one of those times that he surprised me and gave me a bunch of daisies and shyly kissed me on the cheek. I didn't know what to do so, I took the daises, thanked him and returned his kiss on the cheek. I had a major crush on him for a longtime.

I knew that I was like a little sister to him, but I never forgot it, even now that I was seventeen and he had married someone from out of town last year. Tonino was a handsome young man, with dark curly hair and blue-gray eyes. He has grown tall and even more handsome.

I knew I could trust him. I knew he would protect me! We were like family.

It had taken several hours of creeping in the dark, before I reached his house. His home was located in a remote area near the valley of Canneto surrounded by wheat fields. Even so, I made sure no one was lurking about. I barely rapped on the door. He must have been waiting for me; the door opened cautiously as he pulled me aside and said, "They're looking for you. They're everywhere, come." He led me to the barn, which was next to the house a few feet back, where he kept bales of hay and numerous other farm objects. He grabbed an old ladder and told me to go up behind the stacks of hay.

I gladly and gratefully scrambled up the unstable ladder. I knew I could count on him! There was a small window where I could see the moon. The clouds would cover it now and then; it was not a full moon, but just big enough to lend some light to an otherwise pitch black night. I was so tired, and finally I could rest. I felt safe. The day before, they had taken my mother to question her and she hadn't been back.

She had warned me to hide, then wait... and run as far as I could and not to trust anyone; we knew what they did to young women....I was drifting off to sleep when I heard what sounded like muffled, *sotto voce* (in a quiet voice).

I opened the small window and could barely see the side door of the house. There were two large ominous shadows speaking to Tonino, they were here! God help us. Then I heard Tonino whispering, "She's up there," pointing towards the barn.

I moved like lightning, in shock. Barely fitting through the opening of the small window I managed to crawl out and almost lost my footing while closing the window behind me, so they might think I was hiding. At least it would buy me some time. I silently went down the wall while grasping the stones. Thank God it was only a few meters down and thus I was able to escape before they realized I was not in the barn somewhere.

Once down, I began to run through the fields and into the woods behind the wheat fields. The moon was covered and made it possible to hide in the shadows of darkness.

The branches of shrubbery were hurting my skin as I ran through them. Suddenly I realized I left my clothes in the barn, all of them. As if total affirmation of deception wasn't complete, but somehow it didn't seem to matter. The hurt was so unbearable, I felt shattered. "I must not cry," I told myself! But I did! Like never before, I felt betrayed from the one I thought loved me the most!

Gratefully, I woke up!

With tears on my cheeks and the hurt of betrayal, I could still hear him say, *In Sotto Voce!*

(She's Up There...)

(She's Up There...)

Not In Vain

As I LOOK BACK I see it now;
    What foolish years they were
Blindly stumbling through it all,
To find the path to happiness
A tear-stained road I left behind!
A smile or two were there
Along the narrow way.
What shocking story I could tell
But then I shall not be so bold;
Perhaps someday when I am old!
I have seen pain so bare and cold...
Grip happiness I long to hold
Wisdom came to me and left
Alone to face the heavy task
Sorrow and pain were not in vain
I shall not shed a tear!

The Link

IF YOU LISTEN, you will hear!
    Planted seeds of yesteryear
Fleeting visions cast in time
Elusive as a whisper in the night
A remembered fleeting moment
Of familiarity, as if...
I had just been there.
Profound shadows of memories
In its own moment, in time
Then it is no more
If you listen you will feel!
What you know is true and real
Ever so softly Fragments reappear;
Of visions
Long forgotten.
Undaunted, I seek the answer
But alas, It is now gone...
Until tomorrow!

As there is neither a beginning nor an ending.
Leaving behind glimpses of reality past
And taken everything
In its wake of memories vault
From this current moment on.
That comes and goes as it pleases;
Who am I...?
I am; you are a link in a long, long chain.
Connected.
But still in its own circle
Who am I...?
I am
of
Many

The Wave

THE DAY COULDN'T HAVE BEEN more perfect, and I meant to enjoy it fully.

While walking on the beach, I picked up a beautiful flat coral.

This one had strange markings; I'll be sure to look at it later. Along with the coral, I gathered a few intricately carved shells.

After my walk, I settled in my beach chair under the umbrella and gave myself up to the happy feeling of being lulled by sun and surf.

I felt that the birds were there just to entertain me.

I closed my eyes for a few moments. I felt at peace with this beautiful world we live in.

Not a cloud in the sky, with soft breezes caressing me.

In the background, I heard beautiful music of crashing surf from a distance, as in concert, perfectly blending in tune with other sounds directed by nature...as in a dream.

I opened my eyes and saw something in the ocean, someone playing with the waves. As she got closer, I noticed she was young, had long dark hair, and was beautiful.

As she met the wave with such precision, you could see she wore a green iridescent bathing suit that glistened in the sun. She must be an athlete to be able to swim that far, thought.

She waved; was she in danger? I waved back. I was concerned.

I went in the water towards her and loudly called to her:

"Come back! You're too far, come back!" as she disappeared under a large wave! Then I thought: *What am I doing here? I can't swim!*

I had felt a strong, strange compulsion to go to her ...Help her!

And then, suddenly she reappeared high on the crest of the wave. There she was... riding it as if she were part of it.

I was amazed at what I saw next...I could not believe my eyes!

I barely saw a glimpse of a beautiful green iridescent fish tail.

Well, that explains it!

Athlete indeed, I thought as the haunting melody played on in my mind.

The Promise

I WAS SITTING ON something but felt nothing
   It was dark, but I could see...
I was alone... But was not,
Being there felt normal!
I felt a gentle breeze upon my cheek
As if God's breath willed it
I was waiting!
While sitting, I could see us from behind;
Simultaneously, we were both in white
A woman with long dark wavy hair was to my right.
I knew her, but we never met...
Or did we?
We were waiting!
Suddenly as if she had never been...
She vanished... It was her time!
I did not feel cold, warmth, or fear.
I had no questions.
Everything was as it should be
I was waiting!

I saw the Earth! On my right, south;
The size of a walnut; suspended there;
Like a blue jewel! Surrounded
By celestial darkness!
My longing to go back was overwhelming.
I looked up Northwest of where I was
And humbly asked God!
The Creator of all, seen and unseen
To please let me go back!
I asked as a child would ask his father...
I promised, I would do something...
Worthy of my existence!
At that precise moment,
I felt a magnitude glimpse
Of total knowledge;
Everything was clear to me
As never imagined
I knew I was heard!
I knew Him to be.
He knew I was.
I was part of it all!
Words were never spoken...
Then I heard a sweet angelic voice
"You have a beautiful baby girl."
I have told of my experience
To anyone who would listen!
My question is, have I kept my promise?
Note:
I was eighteen, I had a hard labor, and my daughter arrived one month early.
Time is irrelevant.

Roccavivara
(Mena at Eleven)

**Mena at 10 with brothers
Dinuccio and Franchino.**

FROM THE TOP OF THE VILLAGE, you could see the rain coming, long before it got there. The village of San Giovanni across from us was lower and more spread out; when it rains it seems to disappear in the mist.

When they celebrated their patron saint's feast, we could see the spectacular fireworks from here at dusk.

Mother was busy taking down our clothes off the line before the rain started. But that wasn't all; there were rainbows everywhere, whole ones, half ones and pieces of bright colors between the remaining clouds after the rain.

The birds announced their happy concert of sweet chirps after their shower; it was magical! During the month of May we celebrated the Blessed Virgin Adoration Feast. The families that could afford it sponsored at least five prepubescent young girls (I was one of them) or as many as they could afford, to go on a pilgrimage to the valley where the Church of San Canneto is, and where the Smiling Madonna of San Canneto resided. The pilgrimage started early in the morning.

We were led by Signora Severina, a lady from the Church, who was pleasant and very chubby. She wore a scarf on her head, which she tied under her chin like my nonna did, complete with an apron tied around her ample waist.

It took us at least five hours to get to the valley, and five hours to get back. We sang hymns and prayed the rosary, both ways

By the time we started back up, we were all starving.

Some of us pulled dandelions out of the ground and ate them—it was *delizioso* (delicious).

I still like them and cook them the same way, steamed with garlic and olive oil and a dash of salt, like everything else. Is there any other way?

I had embroidered two handkerchiefs—one for the Holy Mother and one for Domenico. Domenico played the clarinet. He was from out of town and played with our band on the feast of St. Emidio. I couldn't wait to see him. After we gave our gifts, we prayed some more, then started back.

Church of Canneto

When we got thirsty we drank water from creeks of spring water, which was abundantly available. Meanwhile our sponsor was busy baking bread and making lasagna noodles for our dinner. The noodles were very wide; the dough was made with semolina, eggs, and water, worked well and stretched out with a long rolling pin then cut into large strips and broken by hand into pieces, then dropped into boiling salted water. When done, it was drained and seasoned with vinegar and olive oil. It sounds horrid; but it wasn't! We lapped that up like little wolves.

Then each one of us was sent home with a large round loaf of fresh bread. Yum...

The bread was baked in a wall brick oven which was made hot manually, and when the interior was hot enough (I still have no idea how they arrived at that conclusion) it was swept clean with long branches of leaves tied around the end of a broomstick. The large wall oven held at least five large round loaves at a time.

The starter, a large cup full of dough, was saved for the next person. No one bought yeast; it was simply just passed on. The aroma was incredible and you could smell it all the way to the piazza and then some. Bread was not sold; everybody baked theirs.

This was Roccavivara.

A few days later, my brothers and many of our friends were playing near the high steps, like a small bridge, dangling our legs when my brother Dino fell over to the bottom and hurt his head. Blood was spurting out all over. We were all screaming and crying. I put my hand tightly on the cut and, with the other arm, I held him tight and started running toward where the doctor lived.

By the time we reached the town doctor, we had at least half the town following us.

We ran past the piazza and past the Church, down the steps on the left with all in tow!

I used to live here when I was very small; I was three and four.

My name is Mena.

I am ten years old. Everyone says that I am bright and pretty. I think they are telling the truth, I have light-brown wavy hair and dark brown eyes. I like looking in the mirror, and sometimes I think I look like my aunt Tany' except she has dark hair. I wish I had dark hair!

I was told it would get darker when I got older.

She was an opera singer and was beautiful, elegant, and glamorous, plus she hugged me all the time. I took my school friend to a Cathedral where my aunt sang the *Ave Maria*; her beautiful voice caressed and filled every comer and curve of the Cathedral! I was so proud of telling my friend that she was my aunt.

Two years ago, my aunt Tany' came to take care of me along with Yolanda and baby Mary, my baby sister, after Papà had been hospitalized. Yolanda was a nice lady. My father met her a year after my mother left. My older brother Cesarino was sent to live with our paternal grandmother in Naples. He always brought me little surprises when he came home from working with Papà. I will miss him.

After a few months, even with my pouting and pleading, it was decided that due to her career which required working late in the evening, I should be sent to live with my paternal grandmother's brother and his wife. I had been there before, but I had only vague memories of it. They were childless and loved children. In fact I was born in their home. My uncle Peppino was a burly, well-dressed gentleman with dark hair and a hint of gray at the temples.

He sometimes wore glasses and had a dark mustache and was stern but kind. I liked him. Aunt Camilla was gentle and loving; she was small and wore her hair in a bun, and I liked her too. I still miss my beautiful aunt.

Grumo is a town west of Bari in the Puglie region which is located on the Adriatic Sea coast in Italy. The streets were made of cobblestone and had a three-globed light post on every corner.

Piazzettas, (small piazza) were everywhere with fountains, gelaterias, and benches under the trees. Piazzas are clearings in the center of different areas of the town where people gathered to socialize and go for *passegiata* (stroll) with family and friends, and someone always played the accordion. This is where love bloomed.

I loved gelato, any flavor.

Soon I settled in my new home. I liked my school and made friends easily. I even helped my uncle develop and colorize photos in the darkroom. The living quarters were in the back. There was something about that room, the one before the darkroom. I had been there before, a long time ago. That's where I had napped! Suddenly I thought of butterflies, and poppies, they are so pretty, strangely I begun to hum a familiar tune.

My great grandfather Francesco Grande, lived here as well, and always had smiling eyes.

He used to tell me stories about magic. I loved him. His job was to grate the cheese before dinner. He would always give me the end pieces which I liked. He hid this transaction from zio Peppino and zia Camilla. We shared this secret like a conspiracy.

The photo studio was in the front. I slept on a divan that converted into a comfortable bed.

On the wall behind the bed were many portraits of all our departed ancestors, including my namesake, my great-grandmother, Filomena. She was dressed in black, as did most of the ladies. It was the custom for mourning. She seemed very serious in a gentle sort of way. Everyone said I resembled her, but they were all wrong. I looked like my beautiful zia Tany.

In the evening my uncle would light a candle on a sconce directly below the photos. When the candle was lit in the dark of night, strange shadows seemed to bring their faces to life with each flicker of dancing light. The lit candle created strange eerie shadows. It would be fair to surmise that they were all waiting for his precise moment to come alive and reminisce about their past and watch over us. They even found their way into my dreams. I felt that they were all looking at me; I studied their faces until it became spooky. At times I felt protected by them; after all, they were family!

Knowing this gave me little comfort though.

When I was frightened, Aunt Camilla said not to be afraid, because they all loved me, but suggested that I pray, and that it would make me feel better. And I did; like never before. I would get down on my knees and pray to the beautiful gesso sacred heart of Jesus. That's when I could feel them all smiling at me approvingly. I smiled back, covered my head, and went to sleep. I prayed a lot that year! When I received my Holy Communion, uncle Peppino took pictures of me, next to the gesso Jesus on a small table.

Aunt Camilla used to take me with her when she went to the almond farm where her relatives lived, to join them in cracking the nuts. We'd all sit around a long table. We'd sing *stornelli* (folk songs) of the region. Plus at the end of the evening, we could take all the almonds we wanted. That was fun.

For many years, my uncle and aunt provided a good home for many children, related or not, in hopes that someday one of us would stay. I would have, until Anna, my embroidery teacher that lived across the street from the studio, asked me if I knew where my mother was. I wasn't sure, but I never really gave it much thought! Of course she must be in Roccavivara. I suppose that having lived with so many different people before Yolanda came to live with us, I adapted, and always felt comfortable with it. For a short time, I stayed in the Sacred Heart of Jesus convent in Reggio Emilia.

**Mamma on the way to the
piazza to fetch water.**

We cleaned, prayed, and sang beautiful hymns all the time, I became friends with a young sister not much older then I was. Well, she wasn't a sister yet, but she was going to be. I did what I was told. My father had told me to always have good manners, be neat, and to always help out, "or else." Well, I certainly didn't want the "or else." So I remembered to do all of those things. I liked it there too. I liked singing in the operetta, Va Pensiero.

**Roccavivara (Commara). Bringing
goats from the field.**

After that, I lived with a family that lived in a beautiful big house in a farm. They had a daughter my age.

We became inseparable friends.

Before Papa' and my brother left, he made sure I stayed with a family with children. It was a good arrangement. They provided a suitable home for me, and in turn, he would take their family portraits. (My brother assisted him in his work). My uncle Gino tutored my brother in his schoolwork, and was quite good at it because my brother was smarter then me, and had a beautiful handwriting. He was my father's younger brother, and was always with us. We loved him.

Base of Roccavivara

Back to the farm; most evenings we roasted peanuts on a peanut roaster on the fireplace embers. (The peanut roaster was much like a long-handled frying pan with holes at the bottom.) I had never tasted anything so wonderful; the aroma filled the house and our tummies. I never wanted to leave.

Anna's words woke up the need in me. I longed to be with my mother and brothers. The next day, Anna helped me write a letter to my mother.

A few days later, I was playing outside with Pietro, (Anna's son), when I saw her; knew her instantly. I flew into her arms; her scent was indescribable! I was home!

I had not seen her in three years, almost four, not since she left with my two younger brothers. My uncle Peppino and Aunt Camilla were furious; I didn't even get to keep my first Holy Communion dress or anything that belonged to me.

I loved them, but I felt I belonged with my mother, no matter where we went. Aunt Camilla tried not to cry—I could tell!

Uncle Peppino didn't say much, almost as if he had expected this to happen.

I promised I would write! (I never did; I wish I had.)

As we were leaving, I saw Pietro. I called him over to me as I pulled my beaded necklace off my neck and gave it to him, to give to Anna.

While waiting for the train to arrive, we ate dark bread and dried figs that she had brought with her for our trip. It was wonderful having lunch with my mamma.

Aunt Camilla was too upset to offer food before we left; it wasn't like her to neglect courtesy.

After the train, we boarded an autobus, then we walked down the valley and up the mountain. We talked a lot, and she asked a lot of questions about my father. I told her about my baby sister and that they were all in the hospital. I don't think she liked the baby sister part. (Now I understand!)

Grumo, Age 10

She still wanted to know everything.

The moon was full and bright so we could see very well in the dark of night. It was almost dawn when we got to the top of the town where I was going to live. I was excited in anticipation to see my brothers and grandparents. The next morning I woke up to two little boys staring down at me. I grabbed them and tousled with them. Let me tell you how those names came to be! Dinuccino was named after my uncle Leopoldo-Leopoldino—Dino equals Leo. Franchino was named after our great-grandfather Francesco, thus Franco equals Franhcino, and of course he is Frank.

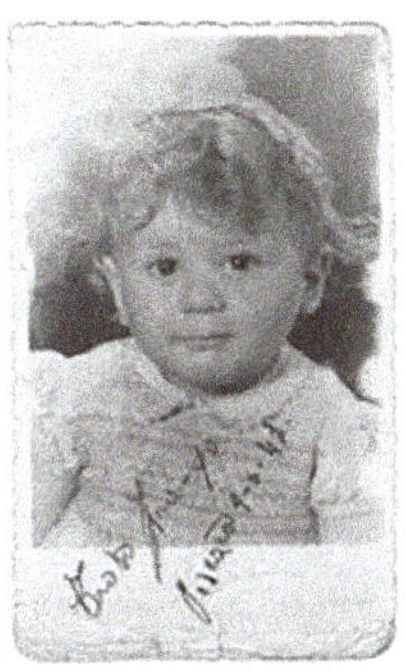

Little brother Franchino

The youngest, Franchino, was chubby and blond like me. Dinuccino a little taller with dark hair and large expressive eyes; they were precious. They were so little three and half years ago. I told them I was their sister and I was going to tickle them so they'd better run. As we burst outdoors, running and laughing, we ran into all our neighbors in front of our door. Mother gave me a chair to sit on so I could talk to everyone to satisfy everyone's curiosity.

I didn't mind! I got to meet a lot of people right away.

We had two chickens. One was white and the other was speckled. They were our pets with benefits. They stayed in our front room where we kept wood for the fireplace. We never saw them during the day, but they always came home at night. I'm not sure when they laid eggs, but when we found them we'd break a hole in them and suck the egg out,— yum!

Sometime when I needed bobby pins or berets, I took whatever eggs I could find to the little store and traded them.

I was where I was supposed to be.

At first it was difficult to understand the dialect, but in a matter of days I could. The Cirulli's (they were the wealthy family of the town) often encouraged my mother to let me spend time with their daughters, Adriana and Italia, because I had good manners and didn't speak with a dialect. In turn they periodically gave mother grain.

I liked where we lived. It was only a few doors from the piazza where there was an ever-flowing fountain.

Hardly anyone had indoor plumbing, except for the Cirullis and other wealthy families. Whenever we needed water, we'd take our large copper container, which looked like a large vase with a curved handle on each side, to the piazza and fill it with water. All the ladies made a donut out of a small towel and placed it on their head for cushion, then placed the large vase on top of it and with their hands on their hips, off they'd go. They'd walk from one end of the town to the other, down the stone steps past the piazza and the Church. I tried that, at first without water then with a little water. I thought it would give me some balance, but nothing worked. I can't tell you how many times I tried! We had more dings on our copper container than you can imagine. Mother never told me to stop trying. But I don't think she knew how many times it fell from my head.

One day we went to visit some friends, and on the way down from the piazza we passed a two story house. I stopped and stared at it; I seemed to remember something about *farfalline* (small butterflies) of blue and gold. It was a sad memory; strangely a song about poppies came to mind and I didn't know why. My Nanna

40

noticed and asked what was wrong. I told her I didn't like that house. *"Perche' piccola?* (Why, little one?) You used to live here, when you were three!"

Nonna lived almost at the base of the mountain. She always wore a scarf on her head and an apron, and of course her clothes were always black, because my uncle had died at war a long time ago so she was in mourning and always would be, like most of the ladies in town. It was almost a required custom, especially when a member of the immediate family died.

Sometimes she walked me home, and on the way up, we'd pick berries on the side of the road and eat them. Other times we would dig out dandelions. They grew everywhere. We'd shake the dirt off of them and put them in her apron and my skirt. When we got home we'd wash them and steam cook them in a pot with olive oil and garlic plus a dash of salt. Of course, in everything we cooked we used garlic and olive oil. The fireplace had a chain with a hook to hang pots. We cooked everything there after we started the fire with kindling wood and a log. Olive oil was used for everything, from cooking, to hair, skin and even to polish leather shoes. I liked the smell of it.

**Grandfather Guiseppe Sallustio with
Ida, my brother Ceasar's wife in 1957.**

We had dandelions for dinner with a big chunk of crusty dark homemade bread, or Mamma would make corn bread, baked on the hearth in an iron skillet! We had a grate over the embers that you could roast or cook on. Store-bought was a luxury we could not afford, nor needed.

Nonna had gray eyes and light graying hair braided and wrapped at the base of her neck as in a bun. She was of medium height and weight, spoke softly, was gentle and moved slowly, like she planned her movements carefully. Grandfather was quiet. He was thin with lots of white curly hair. I don't think I ever saw him standing up, so I never knew how tall he was. He sat in front of the house with his cane.

Great grandfather Francesco Grande

I stayed away from him; the cane intimidated us all. One time he waved it at us when we were playing and making too much noise. Somebody had told me that he didn't like us because he was angry with mother for running off with my father when she was working as a nanny in Vasto, which was arranged and recommended by our town priest. My father was working with his uncle as a traveling photographer, (from Bari).

I spent a lot of time with my Nonna— she had been to America. Mother and aunt Angelina had been born in Bristol, Pennsylvania. Nonna didn't like it there. She said the air was heavy and gave her headaches, so she convinced my grandfather to move back home to Italy. Her sister and husband remained. The sisters were heartbroken to be separated. Each sister had two children. Uncle John simply would not even remotely consider going back to Roccavivara.

He said that they would have a better life in America, and would not give up his job at Campbell Soup Company in Camden N. J. (He was a wise man). My mother was two years old and my aunt was four. She still remembered how to say Gelato, in English. One thing I could not imagine—America had sweet potatoes how could this be?

Maria Grande, Grandmother

Nonna said so, then it must be true.

On the way home from Nonna, I looked for my brothers, but they were nowhere in sight. Maddalena heard me calling them and told me that they had gone home some time ago. Our town was like a big family. When calling my brothers I could hear the echo of different people relating my message, bouncing down between sloping houses in narrow streets.

Maddalena lived behind and below from where we lived. I could see her house from our window, and often I waved at her as she watered her plants on the terrace. I always thought she was pretty. She had long reddish blonde braids wrapped around her head. That hair style was called a braided crown. Her father was a little strange. I heard people say that he was slightly deficient. Every day he went to the piazza and put his head under the cold running water of the fountain. He was thin and tall and had short, curly white hair, and never said much. I often wondered if all that water had made his hair that curly. Sometimes Maddalena let me help her when she made bread, then she always gave me a large round loaf of bread to take home.

Commara Assuntina did the same thing when she made ricotta; she would always give us the water from the ricotta which was called *siro*. That was a treat, with little chunks of ricotta still warm. She was Michelina's *commara*. I called her *commara* because Michelina did, and she was my very best friend. She lived next door. Regardless though, everybody seemed to be somebody's *commara* anyway, but she wasn't mine. Michelina's father was the town sweeper. Many times at night he would sit in front of the house and play the accordion. We would sing *stomelli* (folk songs) and dance 'till it was time to go to bed. Michelina and I were very good at singing. We used to sing all the time.

Someone had said that Assuntina was not my *commara*, but dear *commara* Assuntina came to my rescue and said I could call her that—and I did—all my life!

Back to Madda, as she wanted to be called now that she was not a little girl any more. Most of all, she told me and Michelina what to expect when we became young women. Of course we couldn't get enough of that valuable information, as she recently had become a young woman herself.

She did look different, we thought.

The Rock, *"Rocca,"* as we often referred to our town, also had a town crier. From time to time, we would hear him blow his horn, and we'd run outside to hear what he had to say. He was a tall slim man with a cap and an overcoat with the collar up when it was cold. He held his horn to his side while speaking, *in alto voce.*

Nostalgia

Nostalgia!
    The word alone
Takes me back
To a place in time
A part of me left behind
As a grain of sand
In the wind
Was that really me?
Running into my Nonnas open arms
Drinking the perfume of her
As she held me tight.
These arms have embraced her,
My eyes beheld her;
The memories are real, as
Tears and laughter of yesterday.
Tangibly I am the same;
But not all...of me.
Sometimes I feel detached from myself
From what was and is no more;
Until...I hear whispers of yesteryear
And Feel...! What I felt.
Nostalgia!
Memories become tangled in time...
The hunger of longing
Assault me,
As in a surrealistic dream
Helplessly I surrender to the pull
Grasping golden threads of time

Transporting me back
To a nebulous space
Of
What was...
And always will be.
Holding on tightly to each
Fast fading elusive piece
Of the intricate puzzle
We all know as
"LIFE"
Nostalgia!
Mamma...
She never outright said the words
"I love you"
She didn't have to!
But we knew,
We knew!
How could she have known
All my little secrets?
I would often wonder.
Just the same, I didn't mind.
She was beautiful.
Did I see it then?
Did I smile back in acknowledgment
Of her love?
Surely she must have known.
Nostalgia!
Painful longing to recapture
And relive all the moments
Along with the not so special
Ones.
And is now in yesteryears

Abyss.
Wrapped in the mist
Of time
As pebbles in the snow
You cannot see them
But you know
They are there!
Engulfed in joy and sadness
Simultaneously felt.
That brings tears and smiles
As sunshine thru the rain
Words cannot adequately describe
The longing! Of such magnitude
As we touch everyone on life's journey
I cannot help but wonder
Did I plant seeds of happiness?
Did I trample on delicate
Coloured shells?
Crushing them...
Crushing you!
Nostalgia!
The sound of my brother's laughter
When we were children still rings in my ear.
The first time my baby daughter spoke
Her first complete word
Looking up at me with full acknowledgment
Of who I was
And murmured softly! Mommy!
As she contentedly drifted off to sleep.
The first love
Purity of innocence,

In its purest form.
Feelings of ecstasy
Not entirely understood...
Not forgotten;
So much love!
So little time...

Roccavivara in the mist of dawn.

The Rose & The Baboon

PURE OF MIND and body!
    And with all honesty I say to you,
I am in the spring of my life...
You reply with much candor!
United with veiled cruelty;
"That it is not so, my dear."
A baboon in all its simplicity
Would have been less contrary
In its naked truth
After all; he is but a baboon.
And I say to you, with pure sincerity
That I find the baboon quite pleasing.
After all, he has a rose for me.
You do not!

Drawing by my dear friend Dorothy Rhines

Where Are You My Talisman

THE NIGHT IS DARK and still.
 So weary am I, but yet I know
I must not sleep!
For if I should, fear and terror
Beyond thought await me;
Against my will,
My limbs becoming weak...
Engulfed in your caress
Of velvet darkness.
You pull my being and dull my senses.
I cannot move my hands upon my breast
Though I hear my heart beat fast.
Falling, turning deeper still I fall.
Gripped in fear and horror!
I clinging here remain, with despair.
It is too much for me to bear.

To shout and cry would be bliss.
I cannot shed a tear nor move my lips.
Is this the way to die? Oh no, it cannot be.
My will to breathe is also deaf to my demand.
Where are you, my talisman?
It is so deep in this abyss.
Will I see the new dawn's mist?
Note:
I resisted this malady for many years and suddenly it stopped.

Despair

I SEEM TO FADE, dissipate,
 In this world I longed to love

Happiness indeed would be,
If I no longer lived for thee!

Behind this wall I shall reside;
Don't come near, nor go too far!

Sadness cast her long black veil
I shall linger and survey!

Colors blaze so bare and bold
I reach out, but cannot hold...

Laughter seems to fill the air,
Barely reaching to my ear;

Abandon thee? I shall not!
For I love thee not enough;

I know not love, but what I feel.
Salty tears upon a shattered heart!

That cannot heal...

Till Dawn

I STOOD BY YOUR SIDE:
   As I gently touched your cheek!
The quiet and stillness of the night
Bid not a word to speak!

With trembling fingertips, I drew near and touched
Your moist but silent lips to mine!
My quivering lips tasted salty tears

That dripped from my eyes;
That softly rested upon your face.

I would stay by your side
Till dawn!

Leaving behind kisses so deeply desired;
Shocked, betrayed; I turned to go.
As you lie there so still and silent...
And cannot even utter my name!

Go then, as you must!

All the wrongs will be forgiven;
And forgotten.
All the love will be
Remembered, and
Cherished.
Fare thee well!

Unforgettable

I WILL NEVER FORGET THAT beautiful spring evening at Gold Coast Ballroom. My friends and I had been going there for several years, but tonight something was different. I could feel the magic in the air that it was going to be a memorable evening!

The excitement grew as the dancers began to fill the tables. We changed into our dancing shoes as soon as possible; a moment missed is a moment lost, forever.

The hypnotic music began to play, and magically transformed us all, with impeccable posture of beauty and grace.

The ladies, the young and not-so-young looked elegant and wore appropriate garments, to complement the movements as they danced.

The gentlemen looked grandiose as they approached the ladies, and as they gracefully extended their hand to the lady, for the dance choice, she would smile in acceptance, taking their hand. They never asked, they simply and courteously extended their hand.

We were now ready to enter the world of pure passion and joy that is ballroom dancing, as the music played to its wave of crescendos.

With complete abandon I touched the stars.

I felt elated in knowing that I was exactly where I wanted to be. The evening went wonderfully well, and then I noticed a gentleman doing a beautiful waltz. He was new and I wanted to dance with him Being somewhat of an outspoken nature when it came to dancing, I approached him. His name was Jim, and he had been a priest at one time. He was handsome and just right for my height, with reddish hair and a nice smile. We shared our love of dancing and became very good friends for many years.

It was almost the end of the evening when a tall, dark, and (yes) handsome robust man extended his hand. Walking on air, I smiled and took his hand. To this day I do not recall the exact dance; I simply felt as agile as a feather, pure as an angel, and moved by the gentle touch as he led me into movements I did not know I was capable of. I was filled with the magic of music as I was lifted above him and reached for the sky! Then, gently, I floated down as my cheeks brushed against his face and rested on the curve of his neck, as my feet ever so softly touched the earth beneath me! We were surrounded by many people, but we saw no one as we moved to the magic that was us and music. I was young, beautiful, and with complete abandon, I touched the stars with the passion of the tango.

The purity of ballet and the abandon and vigor of a Viennese waltz! Overcome by the powerful feelings, I became....the feather, the snowflake, the angel, the music. I became all of those things and much more, as I danced like never before or after. Thank you Michael, Frank, Jim and all my dancing friends, for priceless memories!

Pride

I SEARCHED FOR YOU.
We found each other

We loved, embracing life.
We stepped on petals of happiness

Taking, not giving.
I let you go
Hoping you would stay

You did not look back!
You wanted to...

I did not turn around
I should have!

Pride let you go!
Pride did not listen to...
My heart breaking

Perhaps it was not our time
Perhaps it never was!

Pride won,
Love did not...

Just the same,
My heart is broken.

My First Love

THE EXCITEMENT FILLED THE AIR as the day of our town's feast grew near. Saint Emidio is the patron Saint of Rocca. The procession started from the church after Mass, and proceeded thru the street, passing the piazza to the end, at the bend of the road where the cemetery is located. Then they turned around with many worshippers and children following the band and at least half of the inhabitants with rosary in hand joined the procession.

Every year, the band grew as other musicians from neighboring towns joined them. The rich sound of the church bells added excitement in the air as the grand festival went on. The windows of houses were dressed in multiple colorful spreads of silk, satin, and embroidered table covers that were completed for just this holy celebration, and then put back in the dowry of their daughters.

Late in the afternoon, Saint Emidio was taken back to the church with all the honors, prayers, and hymns.

The band was served a voluptuous dinner in the piazza prepared and served by all the ladies of the village. Dinner is always prepared at lunch time, and lunch is served in the evening.

The best was yet to come!

That evening, Cettina, Michelina, and even Madda, joined us at the piazza to dance and partake in the flirting with the new boys in the band. I was happy to see that Domenico was there (he participated last year). We all knew he was my boyfriend!

The band was perched on a stand slightly higher than the crowd, and they all looked handsomely grand in their uniforms, even Armando. He was my friend and was the son of the postman. He was also responsible for the bells of the church, and today he passed that responsibility on to his younger brother.

There was a boy older then we were, even older then Madda. He seemed to be everywhere we went, and every time he got our attention, he touched himself. We all laughed and ran off. Madda had an idea; she told us to get a handful of small stones and hide them behind our back, and we went looking for him. We didn't have to look far; this time he got braver and exposed himself, discretely enough that people around him didn't notice, but he made sure that we did. "Ok, girls let him have it!" We did—before her words were out of her mouth! We bombarded him, *"Ciao, sporcaccione"* which means bye-bye nasty boy. After that, he disappeared.

I saw the boy I liked. Armando had told us last year his name was Domenico, and that he was fifteen years old. He played the clarinet and was very handsome. He had short, light, wavy hair. He was taller than I remembered from last year. I slowly walked over to where he was. I looked up shyly and smiled at him. He saw me and smiled back. I ran off and hid behind my girlfriends. The ritualistic flirting continued through the rest of the day into the evening, till the band stopped and the fireworks began. I coyly hid from him as he tried to find me—behind the fountain, around the corner, behind my girlfriends...then my friends stepped aside and pushed me towards him; we almost touched. They casually stood in front of us facing the onlookers and fell silent!

We stood there not daring to look at each other...not looking away, afraid to, not saying a word for a long time...the nearness was sweet agony, but not long enough; not then—not ever...

I wanted to stand there forever; this moment would always be etched in time, for always and forever in my heart.

Everything felt different; the sounds were softer, the people talking, the fireworks, the fountain sounded far away; but not. Everything felt strong but in a dreamy sort of way. I felt older then I was, and younger at the same time. I felt feelings of so much happiness, almost too much to bear. Domenico became and remained my world.

Mother broke the spell; it was time to go home.

The next morning I woke up early to stand in front of my door to wave goodbye to him as the bus was taking the band and him away. He waved back and blew me a kiss. I did the same.

I knew the bus was going to take some time to get to the bottom of the town, past the cemetery as it followed the curve of the road down and past my Nonna's house.

I ran all the way down between houses. Madda saw me and smiled, she knew where I was going. I got there before the bus and stood in front of my Nonna's house, waiting to wave at him again. When he saw me he broke into a big surprised smile and blew many more kisses in my direction and showed me the embroidered handkerchief I had given him pressed against his cheek! I was so happy and sad at the same time. I cried, *"Ciao Domenico ti amo!"* (He stayed in my dreams, all of my life).

Ten years old.

It Was You

I SAW YOU LAST NIGHT;
  An avalanche of memories filled my senses
Of things that have been or could have been
But never were!
The longing; unfulfilled;
Dreams waiting to be realized...
I saw you, long ago...and then again
In the present time, or not!
In a dream!
It was—you...
Before my eyes beheld you!
I knew!
Before I heard your voice
I knew!
The physical change does not matter!
Time...
Irrelevant!
I feel your presence;
Always!
Undeniably as the forces of nature
Combined to fulfill its destiny
Is it time?
At last...
For us?

Met By The Sea

GRANDEUR WATER OF THE SEA
    Friend or foe, as life
Unfold your arms to my hapless soul.
Wash away the tears that burn my very being
To gently mingle with the vastness of your water;
Oh but we were silly long ago,
I would run to you and laugh...
There I would be met by sea and foam
You would tickle my nose
And roar with laughter!
And with your mighty arms,
You would sweep me home
To safely rest upon the sand.
Among pebbles and coloured shells,
Let us play again as many times before.
Or have you grown old
And lost your sense of humor?
Or is it me?

Dance of Life

YOU WERE SO FAR, FAR AWAY THEN!
    I knew not of you, nor cared.
I danced among flowers and many other
Living things.
I was them, they were me.
I watched them all in pure delight and glee
As we shared each other's beauty and grace
Were you there then?
I lay among a field of red poppies and
Drank of their intoxicating perfume...
I danced with them,
They danced with me.
As we marveled at each others purity,
As a lily freshly sprung
In the mist of dawn;
I had forgotten you were there!
Though I had seen a glimpse of you
Now and then!
You've come closer now...
As I knew you would.
Dance with me now!
And the dance will go on,
Among the stars!

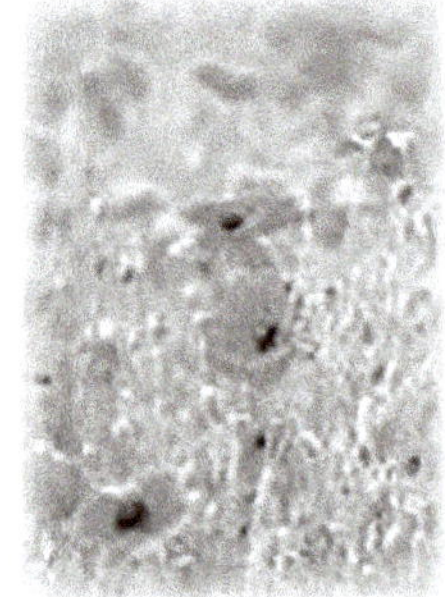

Lovers Lament

UPON MY SHOULDER YOU SHALL REST
As a bird upon its nest!
The empty branches cannot speak
This you know and cannot sleep
You look about and cannot find
What you thought
Was well and fine...

Sweet Repose

RAIN BEGINS TO FALL
　As gentle tears of joy
Bringing children's noses
Against windowpanes
With wonder in their eyes
And sweet repose from play

Procession of St. Emidio

The Bloom of Life

Violets, so much beauty in so few blooms,
    Kissed tenderly by the wind and rain
Caressed lovingly by the sun
And bathed in the morning mist!
Be it only for a while...
For the wind and rain will punish!
The sun will burn.
And mother earth will fold you
In her vast loving arms
Once more
For you have tasted the sweet
Bitter fruit of life;
Be it only for a while!
Am I to bloom in vain?
No, not in vain;
My heart knows...

I Saw It There

I SAW IT THERE, little and gruesome as you please!
   A chubby young naked little demon,
No bigger then a small mouse.
With little horns and a pitchfork
Gleefully looking at me,
With an evil grin....
I was trying not to look at it;
But someday!
I'll rip those tiles right off the wall.
Or better still...
I'd yank that little pitchfork
Out of his tiny, gator-like talon-for-nails hands
And drive it into his gruesome little skull
With horns a plenty.
And hopefully it will not come to life.
At the end of his tiny weapon...
Oh dear, who's the demon now!

He's everywhere!
Etched into the tiles of my bathroom...
Would love to dunk him in holy water
As it wiggles to get free!
Screeching out for his daddy
OH NO!

Relationship

WHAT MAKES A RELATIONSHIP WORK?
Having reached my life to the point of where it is today and after trial and error, I've come up with my own recipe.

No, not tomato sauce for my wonderful ricotta gnocchi or pizza. But for something just as *delizioso*. The kind that makes you smile and lose weight at the same time.

First you will need three major ingredients.

Love, trust, and faith, rolled into one; for smoothness adding a drizzle or two of patience can't hurt, and by adding spice here and there, is very healthy.

Have you ever danced in the rain on a summer day or night?

I still smile when I think about the time we did.

But really, the success of a relationship rests entirely on attitude.

Mutual respect as being the golden key that opens the door to the many facets of a loving relationship.

For some of us it is a learning process.

I have burned some of the best recipes—why? Because I forgot it was on the burner, or I started to do something else while ignoring what was really important.

As for the art of conversation and listening, if you want him to listen to you, then you must listen to him. It is just plain common courtesy. Small talk is definitely not small.

It is also important to look for the good in your partner. This will promote well being and of course it will bounce back to you, trust me.

Basically, even if you have all the ingredients stated above, you must still pay attention... to the way you cook it.

The consequences will promote intense heartburn!

That may or may not be salvaged by self—inflicted damaging behavior.

Depending on how long it took you to realize the damage caused by not stirring it. Plus a strong desire to consciously change old patterns that causes *acido*! (Heartburn).

That's when LOVE steps in, and if the bond is strong enough... Well then *Salute*, (to your health) happy cooking and Enjoy! La dolce vita.

Of Many

To thy many selves be true
There are many to choose from, and it is a choice.
Entities waiting to surface, one by one,
I choose the one most generally accepted by society.
Knowledgeable, composed, pleasant and witty:
Liked by all, no turbulence there!
Until—the child side squeezes past all that composure and
Announces that it's time to have fun, and fun she/he must have!
Fun is good, if controlled.
The composed one will make sure of that.
Then out of the blue yonder, meekly and barely visible
Is the insecure shy one.
Harmless, hardly tolerated by all the others, but accepted.
After all...
It is a piece of the puzzle, and it is needed to complete
The whole persona, hoping that it will go back into obscurity in
the corner of the mind somewhere, sucking its thumb.
And when you least expect it!
The mischievous one, a close friend of the child,
Decides to rock the boat, now this one needs tighter reins
Because it likes to take control!
But never fear: Composed is here...
And it's just the tip of the proverbial iceberg.
But the one that you need to handle with kid gloves as if it were
dynamite would definitely have to be
The angry hateful one!

Full of rage, as a stormy sea, a volcano out of control.
And at that moment, it forgets all that is good.
It took all of them a longtime and determination.
Of working together to keep this malevolent piece of the puzzle
at bay.
And at bay it must be kept...
By chains of nurturing care.
After all they were all one! And one for all!

The Ruins Of Pompei

THE AVENUE WAS A SHADOW of what it used to be, reduced to preserved ruins.

We strolled along, surrounded by remnants of what was left behind.

Half a wall, still standing by marvel of building engineering.

Painted frescos on interior walls of what had been grandiose palazzos.

The next *strada* (street) was what must have been a modest villa; I was drawn to it!

I touched the partial wall and felt a jolt of memories assaulting me, pulling me back in time. Memories from my subconscious mind of a woman who lived here.

I closed my eyes... In my mind's eye, clearly I saw a woman of benevolent nature in her late thirties; my friend and confidant, kind, wise and my anchor of an otherwise unhappy life from an abusing mate.

Her name was Benedetta (which means blessed). I do not recall her name in its entirety, it had a B sound to it and I chose Benedetta because she was truly a blessing in my life. She wore bright colors of golden yellow and blue silk.

Her hair was dark, coiled and tied at the base of her neck, then fell freely to her waist.

I see myself going to see her discretely at times when life becomes unbearable.

Who was this woman? I didn't feel that she was my mother...

Another jolt of vision/memories... I fell and hurt myself! Benedetta was there consoling me, rocking me in her arms, trying to make me smile.

I can still feel her smile caressing away my pain. I felt her presence accompanied by the sudden deep pain of losing her once more as she faded in the mist of time.

Benedetta had been my Nanny!!!

Street in Pompei
Mena

Roccavivara after the
war (Uncle Mario)

**Cessarino
(Big brother)**

Church of Canneto

Church
(Canneto)

Church

Madonna of Canneto

**Mamma making pizza
in America**

A poppy field

Brother Leo "Dinuccio"

We Are

A GOLDEN GLOW BATHED over me,
I felt the warmth of the light gently
Caressing me from within
The aura changed... from
Lavender, to deep purple
Feelings had been forgotten
For a long, long time
How could I?
Even for a brief moment?
But now I knew!
The feelings of precious memories
That time as a thief in the night
Cast her vast black cloak
As if it did not exist.
Feelings, with its mighty arm
Battled time...
And opened the door
Memories flooded back
Crystal pieces as in a storm of visions
Came together
And became part of me
Part of us...
It all seems so clearly now.
Undeniable destiny
I closed my eyes, and opened my heart.
A gentle caress brushed my cheek
You are here!

Our spirits joined as one
Part of you felt the forces of
Fragmented Memories
Reflected into infinity,
As in kaleidoscope of colors.
Of what
Was denied thru time
Except...
For these treasured moments
Coming forth in brief encounters
We survived
The long journey
Just for these moments
I spiritually immersed myself
In long forgotten memories
Of something beyond my present intellect
Grasping the glimmer of golden threads
Of total knowledge denied...
But alas!
A sparkle had faded into the dark abyss
Of time,
As a droplets of water cruelly
Put out the light.
And our past moments
Was nor more...?
As many times before
Until!
For a nano second, the door of time will
Open once more, to welcome us
And
We shall be there!
To drink from the well
Of eternal light

Our spirits joined as one
As we bathe in the golden light
And become part of the infinite
Fulfilling its destiny
For all eternity
At last.

Sogno (Dream)

Mary, the youngest.

Roccavivara

**Uncle Peppino and
Aunt Camilla**

All for Love

L OVE...
A basic need
By all living creatures on earth.
Is it a blessing? Or a curse?
As there are infinite drops of water
In the ocean
So are the phenomena of love
Of different levels.
From infancy to
Adulthood and beyond
The good, the bad, and in between.
All addictive.
All unbearably painful ecstasy
Creating havoc as it seizes you in a hypnotic trance
Of uncontrolled state
Physically as well as psychological
People have willingly perished

Over a lost love.
We are addicted to each other
Songs have been written specifically
For this malady, millions of them
Classic example
The infamous fable of Romeo and Juliet.
Both perished!
The price...worth it?

Leo's Dilemma

LEO WAS ALMOST OUT THE DOOR to go to work when an argument between him and his ex-wife, Rose, flared up out of nowhere. It got out of control, as most arguments will, and harsh words were spoken to the point of no turning back. Leo had had enough. He rushed out of the house, slamming the door on his way. He got into his van and headed to work. A few blocks down the road, the van decided to quit running. He thought, "what now!"

All he needed was for a big bird to fly over his head and crap on him. Oh well, I'll just walk. It's not much farther. I'll come back for the van later, and the walk will clear my head, he thought. While the adrenalin still pumped in his brain, two big thugs stepped in front of him and asked if he had any money. He was ready for this— too ready—almost as if he had wished for it, because he was itching to kick somebody's ass. He stared at them, with wild eyes and fists clenched tight. He replies, "Yea! I got some— and a lot more where that comes from!" He moved a step forward and glared at them, waiting...

Nobody moved. Leo was thinking... "Come on, punks, what are you waiting for?" And said no more.

Then suddenly they ran off, and all you could see was dust in their wake.

"Darn!" He said, and rushed off to work.

Now, Leo is not a big man, maybe five-foot-eight, but he is well built, and they saw in his eyes a volcano ready to erupt, and that's nothing anybody wants to mess with.

Sadly, my brother Leo has since passed away from Parkinson's Disease.

Danger (Dream)
5-31-08

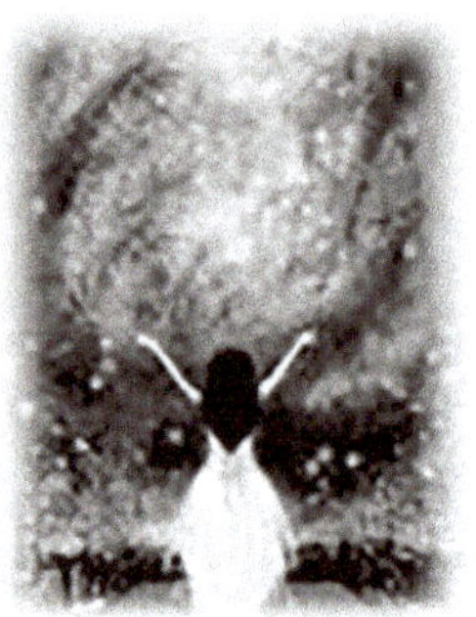

THE FEELING OF URGENCY HIT ME like a crashing wave; I felt I must do something! The earth was in danger. It was moving from its axis...O my God!!! My heart was pounding, my head was exploding with the strong sense of urgency as if a siren went off... pushing me to the next level. I must—I must save it!

In the blink of an eye I was in the vastness of the infinite. I did not feel fear! I was exactly where I was supposed to be. Totally aware of all, where space and time are one; as was I! Part of the galaxy!

I saw the Earth, to my right, in its entire splendor; glistening in the darkness, with blinking stars in the distance. A bright blue round diamond, the size of a perfect grapefruit.

I intuitively extended my hand towards the Earth; then drew it back very carefully.

I could see my arm! I must have been enormous.

I was also aware that my spirit was here. My initial sole purpose was to alert and protect! As if I was the guardian?

I prayed...then I saw a ring of thick fog, slowly surrounding the planet from left to right. To bring balance to an otherwise doomed planet.

At that point I knew that everything was going to be fine.

The creator took care of it!

Note:

I realized I could not hurt the planet by touching it as my natural instinct dictated for I was not tangible.

As stated above, I did not feel fear, cold, warm or apprehension, except for the overwhelming strong sense to protect...it was my purpose.

The dramatic transition from earthly existence to unearthly... was...just was!

It was the most natural development of my existence.

In 1958 while giving birth to my beautiful daughter Venus, I had a similar experience.

(The Promise, page 41*)*

Minus the danger, again I felt compelled to share...needed to share: a must.

I did; so I thought at the time, to everyone that would listen. I owned a hairstyling salon in Roebling, N.J. Most everyone was subject to listen to my experience.

But was it enough?

Again I ask myself... Did I keep my promise?

Anger

ANGER IS THE ULTIMATE TEMPORARY insanity know to mankind.
   Throughout history,in every aspect of life we find
That uncontrolled anger is the cause of many disasters.
Led by wrong decisions, when seized by this malevolent destructive
Emotion: causing irreparable damage
In its quest for dominance!
One must not disturb the sleeping bear in hibernation.
Conditions may or may not be conducive, as the storm
Darkens and begins to swell.
Hardly noticeable as the momentum accelerates!
The eyes become wild...
Surely the inner demon must have been fashioned
To resemble the face possessed, hardly recognizable in its contorted
state
As the infamous Doctor Jekyll and Mr. Hyde.
Upon witnessing the horror of this transformation
It would be wise to run and take cover!

You know it is contagious
You will be part of it!
Without warning like a shot in the dark; it strikes.
And it is too late…to run
A reciprocal malicious wave of unbridled emotion
Has you in its web.
And with a double-edged sword destroys everything in its path.
Even the persona it occupies might not survive in
Its own unprecedented need to conquer and destroy
The ocean was raging, out of control.
("Odin must be angry.")
The Vikings would murmur…
Careful, not to provoke the mighty Odin!
When thunder and lightning created havoc upon the land
Uprooting trees and engulfing dwellings in flames
With a bolt of fire from the sky
It was thought that the Gods were angry;
Very angry.
The vanity of anger does not squelch…
It is lost in its own barbaric need to purge
It knows not how,
Nor does it care…
Do you?

Not forgotten

OF ALL THESE WONDERS, I never tire;
   For they are so precious to behold!

I touch a leaf...So pure and fresh...
A flower so delicately created.

Lost in the oblivion of pleasure,
I shall linger!

To savor the wonder of all, surrounding me.
Within me. ..

Forgotten are the unhappy yesterdays

The sudden realization of all this and more
Filled my heart with rapture.

Tomorrow it may be when I am sad
I may not feel this ecstasy...
So let it be, what it shall!

Tomorrow's yesterday will not be forgotten.
I shall look at all about me; and remember

The beauty my heart so quickly

Had forgotten!

The Man in the Brown Plaid Shirt

LEO RECEIVED A CALL FROM A NEW CLIENT named Bill. He was to meet him in front of a bank not too far from his upholstery shop and then follow him to his house to give him an estimate for his living room furniture. He said his house was complicated to find, and would be best if he wouldn't mind following him. Leo agreed, hung up the phone, and took off to meet him. When he approached the bank, Leo saw a man in a brown plaid shirt getting in his car while nodding at him as a signal to follow him. So he thought. As he followed him, Leo soon found that Bill had been right; it was complicated, with a lot of turns.

The man in the brown plaid shirt didn't make it easy for Leo either, he was speeding like a demon. Leo was having trouble keeping up with him, and was hoping he wouldn't get a speeding ticket. Leo couldn't wait till he got there and get this over with. This man was a nut case.

Well at least Bill (man in the plaid shirt) kept looking back to make sure Leo was following him. After a few miles of turns and running stop signs, the man in the brown plaid shirt parked the car in front of a two-story brick house and ran in, leaving the door ajar.

Leo got out of the van and headed for the house, thinking and hoping it had been worth the joy ride.

"Hello, hello, Bill?"

Bill came storming out of the door with a gun in his hand pointing it at a nervous, frazzled road weary Leo, and with an unsteady voice said "Who the hell are you? Why are you following me, and who the hell is Bill?"

Leo realized what had happened and he then very carefully showed his identification, carefully keeping away from the gun, and explained to Bill or whatever his name was, the best way he could, how things got mixed up. In the end they shook hands. Leo handed him a business card and left.

Now he better hurry back to the bank before the real Bill decides to leave.

www.ingramcontent.com/pod-product-compliance
Lightning Source LLC
Chambersburg PA
CBHW050035040726
47599CB00015B/1686